I0625697

FI MI JAMAICA

LAND OF WOOD AND WATA

WINNIFRED REID

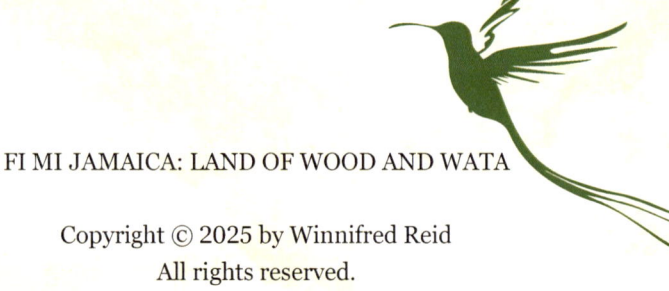

FI MI JAMAICA: LAND OF WOOD AND WATA

Copyright © 2025 by Winnifred Reid
All rights reserved.

No part of this publication may be reproduced, distributed, or transmitted in any form or by any means, including photocopying, recording, or other electronic or mechanical methods, without the prior written permission of the copyright holder, except as permitted by copyright law.
First Edition 2025

ISBN::
Hardcover: 978-1-998245-39-0
Paperback: 978-1-998245-38-3

Cover and book design by Kabrena L. Robinson
Published by Eva-Michelle & Family Publishing
www.evamichelleandfamily.com

DEDICATION

To my 84 year old mama (84 poems)
and my dear grandchildren.

May this collection of poems inspire you to learn about
and appreciate the rich history and culture of Jamaica,
our beloved homeland. May you always remember your
roots and the strong, resilient people who came before
you.

As you grow and flourish, may you carry the spirit of
Jamaica with you, and may its beauty, music, and art
continue to inspire and guide you.

-With love and pride

CONTENTS

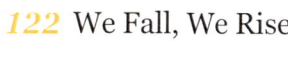

INTRODUCTION

Welcome to this vibrant anthology of poems, celebrating Jamaica's 62nd year of independence! This collection is a testament to the power of poetry to capture the essence of a nation, its people, and their experiences.

Within these pages, you will discover a Jamaica that is both familiar and new—a land of beauty and contrast, where the warmth of the sun meets the coolness of the breeze, and the rhythms of reggae music pulse through the streets.

Through the voice of the poet, *Fi Mi Jamaica* takes you on a journey across Jamaica's landscapes, from the Blue Mountains to the coastlines, and into the hearts and minds of its people. You will encounter poems that explore themes of identity, culture, history, geography, and gratitude, as well as poems that celebrate love, life, and the human spirit.

This anthology is a tribute to Jamaica's rich literary heritage, and a celebration of the island's continued creativity and resilience. Whether you are a Jamaican at home or abroad, or simply a lover of poetry and culture, you are invited to join this journey through the pages of this anthology, and to experience the beauty, passion, and spirit of Jamaica and Jamaicans.

FI MI JAMAICA

Fi mi Jamaica, land of my birth
Where the sun shines bright, and the sea meets the earth
From the Blue Mountains high to the coast so fine,
Jamaica, my home, in my heart, it shines.

In your hills and valleys, I find my rest,
Where the rivers flow, and the bamboo trees are blessed.
Their gentle rustle, a soothing melody,
In Jamaica's embrace, my soul is set free.

Fi mi Jamaica, land of wood and water,
Where the people smile, and its culture is a treasure.
From reggae rhythms to jerk and curry spice,
Jamaica, my love, my heart there.

In your markets, vibrant with colours so bold,
Where the scents of spices and fresh fruits are sold.
The warmth of your people, a welcome so pure,
In Jamaica's arms, I'll abide forevermore.

Fi mi Jamaica, land of beauty and might,
Where the spirit of freedom shines like a beacon bright.
Forever in my heart, you'll stay dear,
Jamaica, my home, my love, always near.

J IS FOR JAMAICA

J is for Jamaica, where the sun shines bright,
dancehall and reggae, rhythms so sweet.

A is for the amber sunsets that blaze,
Mountains and valleys, lush and green.

M is for the mangoes, juicy and ripe,
The laughter of children, so joyful and free,

A is for the ancestors strong and brave,
Through trials and triumphs, they've paved the way.

I is for the island, our treasure and pride,
Where love and resilience always abide.

C is for the culture, rich and profound,
From dancehall to festivals, life is a song,

A is for the spirit, vibrant and bold,
J is for Jamaica, a place we call home!

JAMAICA, JAMAICA

Jamaica Jamaica, land of my dreams
Where the sun dips into the sea, and the mountains beam.
A haven of beauty, where my heart finds rest,
In your lush green hills, I am forever blessed.

Jamaica Jamaica, land of wood and water,
Where the rivers flow, and the bamboo trees chatter.
A symphony of nature, that echoes through my soul,
In your embrace, I am made complete.

Jamaica Jamaica, land of vibrant culture,
Where reggae rhythms, and jerk seasonings capture.
The spirit of your people, a treasure to behold,
In your markets, stories of old are told.

Jamaica Jamaica, land of freedom and might,
Where the spirit of Bob Marley, shines like a guiding star so bright.
A beacon of hope, that guides me through life's plight,
In your heart, I find my peaceful delight.

Jamaica Jamaica, land of my ancestors' pride,
Where the legacy of their strength, forever will reside.
In your soil, their roots run deep and wide,
In your beauty, my heart will forever abide.

LAND OF WOOD AND WATA

Jamaica, Jamaica, a land so bright,
A Caribbean island, full of delight.
Reggae music plays, and people sway,
A cultural heritage, that's here to stay.
From mountains to coastlines, it's a beautiful sight.

Jamaican people, warm and so kind,
Welcoming visitors, all the time.
Smiling faces, and open arms,
A sense of community that disarms.
Respect and love, for each other they find.

Jamaican food, a fusion so sweet,
Jerk chicken and rice, can't be beat.
Ackee and saltfish, a breakfast treat,
Fruits and veg, that can't be beat.
A culinary journey that's fun to repeat.

Jamaican music, a rhythm so bold,
Reggae and dancehall, stories untold.
Bob Marley's legacy, lives on and on,
A cultural icon, forever strong.
Music that inspires, and never grows old.

Jamaican culture, a treasure so rare,
A blend of traditions, that's beyond compare.
A land of beauty, with a heart so true,
A place where love and joy shine through.

PRECIOUS PARISHES

In Jamaica's heart, fourteen parishes shine,
Each one unique, like a precious gem divine.
From Kingston to Hanover, they stretch far and wide,
A tapestry of wonder, where love and joy reside,
An island of beauty, where hearts can hide.

Hanover's hills, where sugarcane grows tall,
St. Elizabeth's plains, where horses gallop and all,
St. James' beaches, where sunsets paint the sea,
Trelawny's cockpit country, where history whispers to me,
A land of diversity, where culture shines free.

Westmoreland's savannahs, where cattle roam and play,
St. Ann's hills, where Marcus Garvey's legacy stays,
Manchester, where cool breezes blow and sway,
Clarendon's river, where fish swim,
And dance and frolic all day.

A land of abundance, where nature's beauty stays.
St. Catherine's plains, where the Rio Cobre flows,
Its rivers and history, where community grows.
St. Andrew's gardens, where Hope blooms serene,
A haven of flora, lush and evergreen.

A land of contrasts, where beauty and peace convene.
St. Thomas' hills, where Morant Bay's history shines bright,
Portland's coastlines, where surfing waves delight and
entertain,

St. Mary's hills, where Oracabessa's charm remains,
Kingston's city life, where music and art flourish and thrive,
A land of creativity, where dreams and hopes come alive.

Jamaica's parishes, a treasure to behold,
A patchwork quilt, of stories yet untold.
From mountains to coastlines, each one a work of art,
A land of beauty and love, that's forever in our heart.
A Jamaica, we love, a Jamaica, we adore.

TREASURES OF JAMAICA: JAMAICAN TOWNS

In Jamaica's towns, so vibrant and bright,
You'll find a world of wonder, and pure delight.
From north to south, and east to west,
Each town has its charm, and its own unique nest.

In Montego Bay, the tourist capital shines,
With Doctor's Cave Beach, and its beauty divine.
The Hip Strip's bustling, with energy and fun,
A place to visit, for everyone!

In Kingston, the capital city's alive,
With culture and music, that'll make you thrive.
Visit the Bob Marley Museum, and learn about his way,
And see the city's sights, each brand new day.

In Ocho Rios, the cruise ships dock with ease,
And the town's bustling, with a friendly breeze.
Dunn's River Falls, is a sight to behold,
A natural wonder, that's worth more than gold.

In Mandeville, the hills are rolling and green,
A picturesque town, with a beauty serene.
The people are friendly, and the vibes are light,
A place to visit, and enjoy the sight!

In Port Antonio, the coast is rugged and grand,
With Blue Mountains towering, across the land.
The town's rich history is a story to share,
And the people's warmth will make you feel welcome there.

In Negril, the sunsets are famous and bright,
With Rick's Café cliff diving, a thrilling flight.
The beach is stunning, with its white sand so fine,
A tropical paradise, that's simply sublime.

In Falmouth, the historic town is a treasure to see,
With its Georgian architecture and rich history.
The town's vibrant market is a colourful sight,
With local crafts and food, a true Jamaican delight.

In Spanish Town, the old capital's charm is found,
With its historic buildings and stories abound.
The town's cultural heritage is a treasure to share,
And its people's warmth will make you feel welcome there.

In May Pen, the market's bustling with life,
With local produce and crafts, a colourful sight.
The town's vibrant energy is a sight to see,
A place to experience, the real Jamaica, wild and free.

In Black River, the river's gentle flow,
Invites you to relax and let your spirit glow.
The town's quaint charm is a treasure to behold,
A place to unwind and let your heart unfold.

In Savanna-la-Mar, the historic town shines,
With its rich history and cultural shrines.
The town's warm people will make you feel at home,
A place to experience the real Jamaica on your own.

Linstead Market, a vibrant sight,
Colors and sounds, a true delight.
Fresh produce and crafts on display bright,
A wonderful sight in the morning light!

JAMAICA'S ATTRACTIONS

Jamaica, land of beauty and grace,
With parishes that showcase a wondrous place.
From east to west, and north to south,
Each parish unique without a doubt.

In Kingston, the capital; we find,
Devon House, with its ice cream so divine.
The Bob Marley Museum, a place to visit too,
And learn about the legend, who sang "One Love" true.

In St. Andrew, Hope Garden blooms with grace,
A beautiful oasis, a peaceful sacred space.
And in St. Thomas, lush green hills meet the morning dew,
Morant's Bay history, a story waiting for you.

Reach Falls, a hidden gem, cascading free,
In Portland lush hills, a natural wonder, for you and me
A tranquil oasis, where nature's beauty shines bright and
carefree,
And the roar of the water, echoes wild and free.

In St. Mary, drift on bamboo down rivers wide,
Then ride on horseback along countryside,
With gentle currents and winding trails,
A Jamaican adventure, that never fails.

In St. Ann, we have the famous Dunn's River Beach,
Where the sand is white, and the water's within reach.
And in Trelawny, we find the historic Falmouth Pier,
A place where cruise ships dock, and visitors appear.

In Westmoreland, we have the beautiful Negril Cliffs,
Seven Mile Beach, where sunset gently drifts.
And in Hanover, Jamaica's charming west coast shines,
Lush green hills and stunning beaches, a paradise divine.

In St. Elizabeth, we have the famous Black River Safari,
A boat tour that showcases the wildlife and the scenery so
irie.
And in Manchester, we find the stunning Mandeville Park,
A place where nature reigns, and beauty leaves its mark.

In South West Clarendon, Milk River's warm waters flow,
Healing properties, a natural wonder we know.
And in all of Jamaica's parishes, we find a land so fair,
A place with culture, beauty, and wonder to share!

JAMAICAN SUNSHINE

Golden sunshine warms my face,
A beautiful day in a lovely place.
Jamaica's beauty shines so bright,
Filling my heart with delight,
Making everything feel just right.

The sun's warm rays on my skin so fair
Make me feel happy, without a care.
I bask in its warmth, feeling so light,
Everything's all right in the morning light.
Jamaican sunshine, pure delight.

The island's vibrant colours all around
Make my heart sing, without a sound.
Green hills, blue sea, and sand so white,
A treasure trove, pure delight,
Filling my soul with joy and light.

In Jamaica's sunshine, I find my glee,
A sense of freedom, for you and me.
No worries, no fears, just pure fun,
Under the sun, the day's just begun.
Jamaican sunshine, forever won.

So let's bask in the sun's warm light,
And let our spirits take flight.
In Jamaica's sunshine, we're free to play,
And chase our dreams, every single day.
Jamaican sunshine, hooray!

JAMAICAN DELIGHT

Jamaica, Jamaica, a land so bright,
A Caribbean island, full of delight.
Reggae music plays, and people sway,
A cultural heritage that's here to stay.
From mountains to coastlines, it's a beautiful sight.

Jamaican people, warm and kind,
Welcoming visitors all the time.
Smiling faces and open arms,
A sense of community that disarms.
Respect and love for each other they find.

Jamaican food, a fusion so sweet,
Jerk chicken and rice, can't be beat.
Ackee and saltfish, a breakfast treat,
Fruits and veg that can't be beat.
A culinary journey that's fun to repeat.

Jamaican music, a rhythm so bold,
Reggae and dancehall, stories untold.
Bob Marley's legacy lives on and on,
A cultural icon, forever strong.
Music that inspires and never grows old.

Jamaican culture, a treasure so rare,
A blend of traditions that's beyond compare.
A land of beauty with a heart so true,
A place where love and joy shine right through.
A cultural heritage that's a gift to you.

JAMAICA'S TREASURES

Jamaica's got treasures, so many to see,
From beaches to mountains, a wonderland to be.
Negril's cliffs and sunsets, a sight to behold,
Rick's Café, where the brave hearts unfold.
An island of beauty, where love never grows old.

Dunn's River Falls, a wonder to explore,
Climbing up the waterfalls, and swimming some more.
Mystic Mountain, where the scenery is grand,
A chairlift ride, with a breathtaking view of the land.
A place of adventure, where memories expand.

Bob Marley Museum, a legend's home so dear,
Learning about his life, and wiping away a tear.
Trelawny's rum distillery, a taste of the best,
Appleton Estate, where the rum is put to the test.
A journey through history, with a spirit of quest.

Black River Safari, a boat ride so serene,
Spotting crocodiles and birds in their scene.
Yallahs Falls, a cascading wonder, so pure and so bright,
A swim in the natural pool, a sunny day's delight.
A connection with nature is ever so right.

Jamaica's treasures, a wealth to behold,
From coast to coast, a story to be told.
A land of beauty, with a heart so true,
A place to visit, and a dream come true.
A Jamaica we love, a Jamaica we adore.

JAMAICAN BEACHES

Jamaica's beaches, a treasure so fine,
Ten special ones, I'll tell you in rhyme.
From north to south, east to west,
Each one unique, and truly the best.

Doctor's Cave, in Montego Bay,
A popular spot, in a major way.
Crystal clear waters and powdery sand,
A perfect spot for a beach so grand.

Negril Beach, on the west coast so fair,
Known for its sunsets, beyond compare.
Seven Mile Beach, with its calm sea,
A great spot for swimming, for you and me.

Dunn's River Falls, in Ocho Rios so bright,
A beautiful beach, with a waterfall in sight.
Climb the falls, and swim in the sea,
A fun-filled day, for you and me.

Treasure Beach, Bloody Bay, and Carlisle Bay too,
Runaway Bay, Long Bay, and Frenchman's Cove in view.
Boston Beach, with its jerk chicken so sweet,
Each beach special, a treat to repeat!

JAMAICA'S MOUNTAINS

Jamaica's mountains, a majestic sight,
Tall and proud, shining so bright.
From the Blue Mountains to the John Crow Range,
A land of beauty, where nature's wonders change,
A treasure trove of secrets to arrange.

The Blue Mountains, a famous sight,
Home to the world's best coffee, pure delight.
A cooler climate, where mist and clouds roam,
A haven for birds, and a place to call home.
Reaching for the sky, at 7,402 feet high.

Dunn's River Falls, a wonder to see,
A cascading marvel of pure glee.
A place of adventure, where spirits soar high,
A natural wonder that touches the sky.
Located in Ocho Rios, a popular tourist spot.

The John Crow Mountains, a rugged delight,
A challenge for hikers, in the morning light.
A place of discovery, where secrets unfold,
A land of mystery, where tales are told.
Rising to 3,900 feet, a sight to behold.

Mount Diablo, a peak so grand,
Standing tall at 4,023 feet, in this land.
A challenge for climbers, with a scenic view,
A place of wonder, where nature's beauty shines through.

Mount Lebanon, a mountain so fair,
Reaching for the sky, at 3,970 feet with care.
A place of beauty, with a rich history too.

A place of wonder, where nature's beauty shines.
Mount Charles, a peak so high,
Touching the clouds, at 4,134 feet in the sky.
A challenge for climbers, with a breathtaking view,
A place of wonder, where nature's beauty shines through.

Mount Horeb, a mountain so divine,
Standing tall at 3,970 feet, a sight so fine.
A place of beauty, with a rich history too—
A site of the famous Mount Horeb Coffee Plantation,
It's true.

Mount Catherine, a peak so rare,
Reaching for the sky, at 4,047 feet with care.
A challenge for climbers, with a breathtaking view,
A place of wonder, where nature's beauty shines through.

Mount Sinai, a mountain so grand,
Standing tall at 3,970 feet, a sight to expand.
A place of beauty, with a rich history too—
The site of the famous Mount Sinai Coffee Plantation,
It's true.

Each mountain unique, with its own charm,
A treasure trove of wonders to disarm.
A land of beauty, where nature's secrets unfold.
Jamaica's mountains, a sight to behold.

BLUE MOUNTAIN HIGH

Blue Mountain rises, up in the air,
A majestic sight, beyond compare.
Green and lush, with trees so tall,
A haven for birds and a sight to enthrall.
A mountain of wonder for one and all.

The air is crisp, the wind is light,
A perfect place for a delightful sight.
The trees sway gently in the breeze so sweet,
A haven for nature where love and joy meet,
A place of peace where hearts can greet.

The mountain's slopes are green and wide,
A canvas of beauty where nature resides.
The flowers bloom in every hue,
A rainbow of colors for me and you,
A treasure trove of wonder anew.

In Blue Mountain's heart, a secret lies,
A world of wonder where magic never dies.
A place of dreams where imagination grows,
A haven of peace where love forever glows,
A sanctuary where the heart finds repose.

So let's climb high to Blue Mountain's peak,
And let our spirits with joy and love speak.
For in this special place, we find our glee,
In Blue Mountain's wonder, we are free to be,
In harmony with nature, wild and carefree.

JAMAICA'S VALLEYS

Jamaica's valleys, a sight to see,
Green and lush, a wonder to me.
From the hills to the sea,
A land of beauty for you and me,
A place of adventure for all to be.
The Cockpit Country, a valley so rare,
Unique landscape, with limestone hills to share.
Home to the Maroons, with a history so grand,
A place of wonder where culture and nature expand.
Visit the Maroon Museum to learn and explore.
The Martha Brae River, a valley so fair,
A place of beauty, with a scenic air.
Take a rafting trip on the river so calm—
A popular spot for a fun-filled day to balm.
Enjoy the scenery and the sun's warm rays.
The Rio Grande Valley, a sight to behold,
A place of wonder where nature's beauty unfolds.
Home to the Rio Grande River, with fish and more,
A site of the famous Rio Grande Waterfalls, a sight to adore.
Take a hike or bike ride through the scenic trails.
The Liguanea Valley, a valley so bright,
A place of wonder where nature's beauty takes flight.
Home to the University of the West Indies, a hub of learning,
A site of the famous Liguanea Plains, with a rich history
that's yearning.
Visit the Bob Marley Museum to learn about his life and
legacy.

JAMAICAN COUNTRYSIDE WONDER

In Jamaica's countryside, so green and wide,
You'll find beautiful hills, where rivers reside.
The Blue Mountains rise, with peaks so high,
A sight to behold, as the sun passes by.

The countryside's home, to many a tree,
Like the mahogany, and the cedar, you see.
The mango and coconut, grow plentiful and tall,
A delicious treat, for one and all.

In the hills and valleys, you'll find lovely sights,
Like waterfalls and rivers, shining so bright.
The countryside's where,
You'll find most of Jamaica's farms,
Growing yams and sweet potatoes, and other
Tasty charms.

The Jamaican countryside, is a wonderful place,
Where nature's beauty, shines upon every face.
So come and visit, and take a look around,
You'll love the countryside, as its beauty abounds.

In Jamaica's countryside, you'll find a special charm,
A place where nature's beauty, will disarm.
So come and experience, the beauty of the land,
And take home memories, of countryside land.

JAMAICAN WATERFALL

Jamaican waterfalls, a sight to see,
Cascading down, wild and free.
In the hills and mountains, they flow and play,
Creating a spectacle, every day.

Dunn's River Falls, a famous sight,
A beauty to behold, a pure delight.
Climbing up the rocks, a fun adventure too,
An experience so cool, for me and you.

Konoko Falls, a hidden gem so rare,
A secret paradise, beyond compare.
Surrounded by lush green, and a mist so fine,
A tropical haven, all the time.

Jamaican waterfalls, a source of pride,
A natural wonder, that won't subside.
Flowing from the heart, of the island it's true,
A beauty so pure, for me and you.

Mayfield Falls, a wonder to behold,
A sight so breathtaking, a story to be told.
In the hills of Jamaica, where the water flows free,
A magical experience, for you and me.

Waterfalls and rivers, a treasure so fine,
Supporting life and nature, all the time.

Home to fish and birds, and a sight to see,
An ecosystem so vital, for you and me.

Jamaican waterfalls, a sight to explore,
A world of wonder, and a beauty to adore.
So come and visit, and take in the view,
An experience so unforgettable, for me and you.

In the beauty of nature, we find our peace,
A connection to the earth, our souls release.
So let's cherish and protect, these wonders so rare,
For future generations, and show we care.

JAMAICA'S MINERAL BATHS

Jamaica's mineral baths, a natural sight,
Healing waters soothe the body and feel just right.
Rich in minerals and a history so grand,
A place to relax on this island.

Milk River Bath, a wonder to see,
A warm and creamy mineral spree.
High in calcium and magnesium too,
Good for your bones and your body renew.

Bath Fountain, a bath so fine,
Warm waters that relax in no time.
Rich in sulphur and minerals galore,
Healing properties forever in store.

Rockfort Mineral Bath, a treat so rare,
Warm waters flowing with minerals to share.
Good for your skin and your mind too,
A natural remedy for me and you.

Jamaica's mineral baths, a gift so true,
A natural wonder for me and you.
So come and soak in the warm waters clear,
And let your muscles relax without a fear.

The waters flow from the earth below,
A natural wonder for all to know.

Jamaica's mineral baths, a treat so fine,
A place to unwind, and let your worries decline.

The minerals work, to heal and repair,
Restoring balance, calming the air.
Nourishing body, mind and soul with care,
Leaving you refreshed and renewed beyond compare.

In this tranquil space, your heart will unwind,
Your spirit will lift, and your soul will shine.
In the warmth of the water all cares left behind,
Jamaica's mineral baths, they're one of a kind.

JAMAICA'S RIVERS

Jamaica's rivers, a treasure so fine,
Flowing through the island, like a shimmering vine.
From the mountains to the sea, they wind and sway,
A source of life and joy, every single day.
A gift from nature, in every single way.

Martha Brae River, in Trelawny's heart,
A popular spot, for a fun-filled start.
Rafting and swimming in its calm waters so bright,
A day of adventure in the sun's warm light.
A memory to treasure, a pure delight.

Black River, in St. Elizabeth's pride,
A haven for wildlife, where nature resides.
A place of beauty, where the heart can roam,
A source of wonder, in every single home.
A treasure to cherish, a gift to call our own.

Rio Grande River, in Portland's embrace,
A river of wonder, in a scenic place.
Surrounded by hills and a lush green shore,
A haven for fish, and a sight to explore.
A treasure to behold, forever in store.

Other rivers flow through Jamaica's land,
Like the Milk River and the Rio Minho's grand,
The Wag Water River, and the Spanish River too,
The Yallahs River, and the Hope River anew.
Each one a treasure, a gift for me and you.

RIO COBRE RIVER: RIVER OF WONDER

Rio Cobre River, a sight to see,
Located in Jamaica, a land of glee.
It's the longest river on the island so fair,
Stretching 32 miles, with a history to share.

It starts in the hills, where the water flows free,
And winds its way down to the sea.
Through the scenic valleys and the lush green hills,
The Rio Cobre River, with its beauty fulfills.

It's home to many fish and other creatures too,
Like crocodiles and birds that live in groups.
The river's waters are cool and clear,
A perfect place for a swim with care.

The Rio Cobre River has a rich history as well,
It was used by the Taino people, who lived in the shade.
They used the river for transportation and trade,
And it played a big role in their daily parade.

The river's banks are lined with trees so tall,
And the sound of the water is a gentle call.
It's a place for relaxation and fun in the sun,
The Rio Cobre River is a joy for everyone!

In the river's waters, you can swim and play,
Or take a boat ride, on a sunny day.
You can learn about the river's history and more,
At the Rio Cobre River, there's always something in store!

The Rio Cobre River, a special place we need,
With its beauty and wonder, a treasure indeed.
So come and visit, and take a look around,
The Rio Cobre River, is a treasure found!

OCHO RIOS: TROPICAL TREAT

Ocho Rios, a town so fair,
Located on the coast, with a beautiful air.
A popular destination for tourists to play,
Where the sun shines bright, every single day.

Dunn's River Falls, a sight to see,
A beautiful waterfall, that's a wonder to me.
Climb up the rocks, and feel the water's might,
A refreshing experience, that's pure delight.

Mystic Mountain, a place so high,
Where the views are breathtaking, and the air is dry.
Take a chairlift ride, or zip line with glee,
And see the town of Ocho Rios, from a different height.

Chukka Cove, a place for fun and play,
Where horses and dogs, will brighten your day.
Take a horseback ride, or pet a dog with care,
And enjoy the beautiful scenery, that's beyond compare.

Ocho Rios, a town so dear,
Where the people are friendly, and the vibes are clear.
Visit the craft market, and buy some souvenirs too,
And take a piece of Jamaica, back home with you.

Shaw Park Gardens, a place so serene,
Where the flowers bloom, and the trees are green.

Take a leisurely walk, and enjoy the peaceful air,
And let your worries fade away, without a single care.

Turtle Beach, a place for fun in the sun,
Where the sand is white, and the water fun.
Swim and play, and build sandcastles high,
And enjoy the beauty, of the Caribbean Sea so wide.

Ocho Rios, a town so true,
Where the attractions are many, and the fun is new.
Visit this beautiful town, and have a blast so free,
And take home memories, that will always be with thee!

MOBAY MAGIC

Montego Bay, a city so bright,
Located on the coast, with a beautiful sight.
Doctor's Cave Beach, a place to play,
Where the sand is white, and the palm trees sway.

Montego Bay, a city so dear,
Where the people are friendly, and the atmosphere's clear.
Crystal waters meet the sandy shore,
And the rhythm of reggae, forever roar.

Montego Bay Marine Park, a treasure to see,
A protected haven, for marine life to be
With coral reefs thriving and fish swimming free,
A snorkeler's paradise, for you and me.

The Hip Strip, a place to be,
Where music and fun, are a part of the sea.
Marguerites Jamaica, a place to dine,
Where the fish is fresh, and the vibes are fine.

Cornwall Beach, a gem by the sea,
Soft white sand and calm waters, a sight to see.
With palm trees swaying gently, in the ocean breeze,
A tranquil haven, where worries ease.

Rose Hall Great House, a mansion of old,
With secrets and stories of tales yet untold.

The legend of Annie Palmer, a woman so cold,
A haunted history, that never grows old.

Montego Bay, a city that's a work of art,
Where the beauty of nature will capture your heart.
Visit this lovely city, and let the charm begin,
And let the beauty of Montego Bay forever spin within.

JAMAICAN ANIMALS

In Jamaica's hills and forests deep,
Live a world of animals, in a secret keep.
The Jamaican boa, a snake so grand,
Lives in the trees, with a gentle command.

The hummingbird, with feathers bright,
Flies around flowers, with a swift flight.
Its tiny beak, sips nectar with glee,
A sweet delight, for you and me.

The gecko lizard, with eyes so wide,
Crawls on walls, with a gentle stride.
Its tiny feet, stick to the ground,
A clever trick, all around.

The mongoose, with fur and eyes so soft,
Prowls around through day and night.
Its long tail, balances with grace,
A nimble climber, in its secret place.

The crocodile, with jaws so strong,
Lives in the river, all day long.
Its scaly skin, shines in the sun,
An ancient creature, having fun.

The agouti, with fur so bright,
Roams through the forest, with a gentle might.

Its large eyes, shine like the night,
A curious creature, a wondrous sight.

The butterflies, with wings so wide,
Flutter and flutter, with a gentle pride.
Their colourful wings, shine like the sun,
A beautiful sight, for everyone!

DOCTOR BIRD

In Jamaica's woods, a bird so grand,
The Doctor Bird, with a beak so planned.
It's long and curved, like a doctor's tool,
Helping it feed on nectar so cool.

Its feathers shine, like a rainbow's hue,
Green, yellow, and blue, a sight anew.
It flutters by, at a gentle pace,
A beauty to see, in its natural place.

This bird is special, with a unique song,
A melody sweet, that lasts all day long.
It's oh so special, it has a unique call,
A sound so sweet, would echo through the hall.

In Jamaica's mountains, it makes its home,
Where the air is cool, and the water does flow.
It sips from flowers, with a tongue so strong,
Drinking in sweetness, all day long.

The Doctor Bird, a symbol so dear,
Of Jamaica's beauty, and its culture so clear.
A sight to behold, a wonder to see,
Only found in Jamaica, our National bird.

JAMAICAN PEOPLE

Jamaican people, a nation so bold,
With a history rich, and a story to be told.
From African roots, to a Caribbean shore,
We've got a culture, that's unique and more.
We're known for our music, a rhythm so sweet,
Reggae and dancehall, can't be beat.
Bob Marley and Peter Tosh, legends in our land,
Their music lives on, hand in hand.
Our food is delicious, a culinary delight,
Jerk chicken and rice, a flavour so right.
Ackee and saltfish, a breakfast treat,
Fruits and veggies, can't be beat.
We're a people proud, with a spirit so free,
Our resilience, is a wonder to see.
We've faced challenges, but we always stand tall,
And we'll keep on rising, never to fall.
So let's celebrate, our Jamaican pride,
A people so warm, and hearts filled with joy inside.
We'll keep on shining, like a beacon so bright,
Jamaican people, we're a treasure alright!

OUT OF MANY, ONE PEOPLE

Out of many, one people we stand,
A nation united, hand in hand.
From diverse roots, we've grown as one,
Our differences, now our greatest strength, forever won.

We've risen from the ashes of our past,
Our resilience, forever to last.
We've embraced our cultures, our beliefs, our creeds,
And from our diversity, a new nation proceeds.

Out of many, one people we've become,
A fusion of flavours, a melting pot, where love has won.
We've learned to celebrate, our differences with pride,
And in our unity, we've found our stride.

We're a people of passion, of fire and flame,
Our spirit's strong, our hearts will proclaim.
We're a people of courage, of strength and of might,
Together forever, in the dark of the night.

Out of many, one people we proudly say,
A nation of one love, where all can play.
No matter our differences, we're all the same,
In Jamaican's heart, we're all one people, one aim.

Our motto's a promise, a pledge to our land,
To stand together, hand in hand.
We'll keep moving forward, as one people, as one heart,
And our unity will never depart.

In Jamaica's embrace, we find our strength,
A nation of one people, where love is unbent.
We'll keep celebrating, our differences with pride,
And our motto will be our guide.

We've got a voice that's loud and clear,
A message of hope, that we hold dear.
We're a nation of dreamers, of doers, of might,
We're Jamaica, and we're shining bright!

JAMAICANS AROUND THE WORLD

From the beaches of Montego Bay,
To bustling streets where city lights play,
Jamaicans rise and spread their wings,
Their unique presence forever sings.

In every corner of the globe, they stand,
With strength and pride, hand in hand.
From London to New York's busy pace,
They bring a touch of home, a smiling face.

Through the rhythms of reggae, their culture flows,
In dance and song, their heritage grows.
In kitchens far and wide, the spices tell,
The stories of Jamaica, where memories dwell.

With hearts full of joy and faces bright,
They share their light, a guiding sight.
In times of challenge, they stand strong,
Together in unity, where they belong.

Innovators, dreamers, leaders, and friends,
Their influence and kindness never ends.
In communities vast, their presence is felt,
A testament to the land where they once dwelt.

Jamaicans around the world, shining so true,
Showing a piece of the island, in all they do.
Their legacy lives on, near and far,
A vibrant tapestry, like a shining star.

JAMAICAN LEADERS

Alexander Bustamante, a pioneer so fine,
Led Jamaica to independence—a dream divine.
He fought for workers' rights and a fairer day,
A true leader in every single way.
A founding father of our nation's pride.

Norman Manley, a champion of justice so bright,
Fought for equality, a beacon of light.
He led the PNP with a heart so true,
A statesman and leader through and through.
A legacy of progress for me and you.

Michael Manley, a leader of vision so grand,
Introduced social reforms across this land.
Free education and healthcare for all to share,
A champion of the people, with a heart so fair.
A legacy of love that will forever be there.

Edward Seaga, a leader of innovation so bold,
Introduced technology to young and old.
A pioneer in finance, with a heart so light,
A leader in progress through day and night.
A legacy of growth that shines so bright.

Andrew Holness, a leader of today so dear,
Continues the legacy with a heart so clear.
A focus on education and a brighter future too,
A leader for the people with a heart that's true.
A legacy of hope that will forever shine through.

JAMAICA'S HEROES

Marcus Garvey, a leader so grand,
Fought for justice and a nation's hand.
He stood for unity and a brighter day,
A true pioneer who paved the way
For equality and rights in every single way.

Norman Manley, a champion of the people's cause,
Fought for independence and a nation's applause.
He stood for unity and a brighter day,
A leader and statesman in every single way.
For a better Jamaica, he showed us the way.

Alexander Bustamante, a hero of the land,
Fought for workers' rights and a fair hand.
He stood for justice and a nation's pride,
A pioneer and leader who never stepped aside.
For a fairer Jamaica, he never divided.

Nanny of the Maroons, a heroine so bold,
Fought for freedom and justice, never to grow old.
Samuel Sharpe, a Baptist minister so brave,
Fought for emancipation and a nation he saved.

Paul Bogle, a hero who stood up for what's right,
And George William Gordon, who fought with all his might.
Jamaica's heroes, a shining light,
Guiding us forward, day and night.

Their legacy lives on, forever in our hearts,
A reminder of courage—they played their parts.
Let us celebrate our heroes in every single way,
Honoring their spirits each and every day.

THE LEGENDARY BOB MARLEY

Bob Marley, a legend so rare,
A musician, singer, and songwriter beyond compare.
Born in Jamaica in the year 1945,
A life of music that would soon come alive,
With a message of love that would never subside.
He grew up in Trenchtown, a neighborhood so dear,
With a passion for music that would bring him near
To the hearts of people all around the world,
With songs like "One Love" that would unfurl
A message of unity that would never grow old.
He formed the Wailers, a band so tight,
With Peter Tosh and Bunny Wailer—a story to excite.
They sang of freedom and equality too,
With a rhythm and beat that would see them through
To the top of the charts, with a sound so new.
Bob Marley's music, a gift to us all,
A legacy that lives on, standing tall.
He sang of redemption and a better day,
With a voice that whispered, "Don't give up the fight,
okay."
A hero to many in every single way.
His music lives on, a testament to his name,
A shining star that will forever remain.
Bob Marley, a legend so grand,
A beacon of hope when it was dark in the land,
Guiding us forward with music that's grand.

ISLAND VOICES:
THEN AND NOW

Voices sweet as the island breeze,
Rhythms that make the heart sway with ease.
From Trenchtown to the world outside,
Jamaican singers—their talent cannot be denied.

Bob Marley's legacy lives on and on,
A prophet of peace, his songs still strong.
Peter Tosh's fiery passion, a burning flame,
Burning Spear's soulful voice, a timeless claim to fame.

Gregory Isaacs' smooth, sultry tone,
Dennis Brown's soulful melodies, all his own.
Toots and the Maytals' ska and rocksteady beat—
A legacy of music that cannot be beat.

Marcia Griffiths' powerful, soaring voice,
A queen of reggae, a heartfelt choice.
Bunny Wailer's rhythmic, rootsy style,
A true original, all the while.

But that is not all; there's a new wave too—
Younger singers with talent shining through.
Shaggy's boombastic beats, a party in store,
Buju Banton's soulful sound leaves us wanting more.

Chronic Law's lyrical flow, a rising star,
Jahmiel's melodic voice, near and far.
Alkaline's energetic vibe, a youthful zest,
Jamaican singers, still at their best.

From old to new, the talent never fades,
Jamaican singers, their music never jades.
A cultural heritage, that's forever bright,
Jamaican singers, shining with all their might!

USAIN BOLT:
A CHAMPION'S STORY

Usain Bolt, a runner so fine,
From Jamaica, where the sun always shines.
He's the fastest man, in the world, you see,
And his records, are a wonder to me!

He was born, in a small town, called Trelawny,
Where the people, are warm, and friendly, you'll see.
He grew up, with a love for sports, and play,
And his talent, was evident, every single day!

He started running, when he was just a youth,
And his coaches, saw his potential, and truth.
They trained him hard, and he worked with all his might,
And soon he was, a world-class sprinter, in flight!

He won his first gold, in the Olympics, you know,
In Beijing, China, where the world was aglow.
He ran the 100m, in a world-record time,
And the crowd, went wild, in a joyful rhyme!

He's won many medals, and broke many records too,
And his name, is known, by me and you.
He's a hero, in Jamaica, and around the world,
And his legacy, will forever unfurl!

Usain Bolt, is a name, that's synonymous with speed,
And his achievements, are a wonder, indeed.
He's inspired many, with his talent and grace,
And his love for running, has taken him to his place!

He's a role model, for young and old,
And his dedication, is a story to be told.
He's shown us all, that with hard work, and might,
We can achieve greatness, and shine so bright!

So let's celebrate, this champion, and his name,
And remember his achievements, and his fame.
For Usain Bolt, is a hero, in every way,
And his legacy, will live on, day by day!

MISS LOU

Miss Lou, a treasure so rare,
A Jamaican icon with a heart so fair.
She sang and danced with a twinkle in her eye,
A true cultural ambassador passing by,
Leaving a legacy that will never die.

With her humour and wit, she won our hearts,
A master of words that set us apart.
Her poetry and songs, a reflection of our pride,
A true champion of culture, gliding with stride—
A shining star that will forever reside.

Her music and art, a gift to us all,
A way of expressing the Jamaican call.
With *Ring Games* and *Anancy Stories* too,
She kept our heritage alive and anew—
A cultural treasure forever shining through.

Ring Ding on TV, a favourite show,
Children gathered 'round, their eyes aglow.
Miss Lou's humour and charm, a treat to see,
A cultural icon bringing glee to you and me.

A Jamaican legend in every single way,
Her legacy lives on—a beacon so bright,
Inspiring generations, day and night.
A true cultural icon, shining like a light,
Guiding us forward with her poetry and delight.
A shining star that will forever sparkle with joy.

KAMALA HARRIS: JAMAICAN ROOTS OF STRENGTH

A trailblazer, a leader true,
Kamala Harris, with a heart that shines through,
From Oakland's streets to the Senate's floor,
She fights for justice, forevermore.

With roots that stretch from Jamaica's shore,
Where her father's heritage forever soars,
And India's spice, where her mother's roots entwine,
A fusion of cultures, a spirit divine.

With passion and conviction, she stands tall,
A champion for the voiceless, one and all,
Her spirit unbroken, her will unshaken,
A shining star, for freedom she has spoken.

Through the halls of power, she makes her way,
A woman of colour, paving a new day,
Breaking barriers, with each step she takes,
A true icon, for future generations' sake.

With intelligence and grace, she leads the way,
A beacon of hope, for a brighter day,
Kamala Harris, a name that will shine bright,
A hero for justice, a powerhouse of might!

JAMAICAN PARENTS

Jamaican parents, loving guides,
Teaching their children, with gentle pride.
Values and morals, they instill with care,
Helping them grow, with a love that's rare.

They teach their kids, to respect and obey,
To honour their elders, every single day.
To work hard and study, with diligent might,
And to always strive, for what is right.

Jamaican parents, a supportive team,
Cheering their children on, through every dream.
They encourage and motivate, with a loving tone,
Helping them reach, their full potential unknown.

They share their culture, and their history too,
Teaching their kids, about their heritage, it's true.
From reggae music, to rice and peas and jerk,
They pass down traditions and never shirk.

Jamaican parents, selfless love they show,
Putting their children first, as they grow and grow.
With devotion so strong, and hearts so true,
They are the rock that their children lean on, as they pursue.

JAMAICAN CHILDREN

Jamaican children, a joyful sight
Playing outside, with smiles so bright
Their laughter echoes, through the island air
As they chase each other, without a care

They love to play, with a ball or kite
Flying high in the wind, with pure delight
Their imaginations soar, as they run and play
Creating adventures, in their own special way

Jamaican children, with curious minds
Learning their culture, where history binds.
Dancing to rhythms of reggae and ska,
Embracing their heritage, near and far.

With stories of ancestors, tales of the sea,
In the heart of the island, they learn to be free.
Through laughter and play, they cherish each song,
In the colours of life, where they all belong.

Exploring the beaches, the mountains so grand,
With each step they take, they're proud of their land.
From the warmth of the sun, to the cool evening breeze,
Jamaican children grow, like the tall swaying trees.

With dreams that are bright, and spirits that soar,
They honour their roots, and seek to learn more.
In the heart of Jamaica, their journey begins,
With culture and joy, where true life never ends.

Jamaican children, precious gems so rare,
A joy to their families, and their community to share.
Their smiles and laughter, bring joy all around
A sweet reminder, of the happiness found.

UNYIELDING SPIRIT:
THE STRENGTH OF JAMAICANS

In the heart of the Caribbean Sea,
Lies a land of strength, a vibrant place.
From the mountains high to the golden shore,
The spirit of Jamaica is rich and pure.

In every beat of the reggae drum,
The pulse of resilience, it does hum.
Through trials and hardships, they stand tall,
With courage and hope, they face it all.

Their hearts are filled with unyielding pride,
In unity and love, they do abide.
From Bob Marley's tunes to Bolt's swift stride,
The strength of the people cannot hide.

In fields of sugar and waves of cane,
They've worked with grit, through joy and pain.
Their roots run deep, their stories strong,
In every soul, a vibrant song.

With warmth and laughter, they embrace,
A heritage rich with a vibrant grace.
Jamaicans proud and true,
Show the world what strength can do.

From Kingston's streets to Negril's sands,
They lift each other with helping hands.
In the face of storms, they do not sway,
For the strength of Jamaicans shines every day.

JAMAICA'S BOBSLED DREAM: SUN, SNOW, AND SPEED

On icy tracks, they made their mark,
A tropical team with a chilly spark.
Jamaica's bobsled crew, a sight to see,
Speeding down the mountain, wild and free.

With helmets buckled and spirits high,
They rode the bob with a determined sigh.
Through twists and turns, they made their way,
Their Caribbean flair shining bright each day.

From *Cool Runnings* fame to Olympic might,
They've shown the world their spirit and light.
With every run, a story unfolds—
Of courage, strength, and a nation's pride untold.

Their bobsled dreams, a beacon bright,
Inspiring generations, day and night.
Jamaica's team, a symbol true,
Proving that with heart and grit, dreams come through.

So here's to the team that dared to try—
With every run, they touched the sky.
Their legacy lives on, forever bold:
Jamaica's bobsled team, a story to be told.

THE NATIONAL STADIUM: WHERE HEROES ARE MADE

In Kingston's heart, a stadium stands tall,
The National Stadium, a sight to enthral!
With seats for thousands, it's a grand sight,
Where athletes gather, to shine so bright!

Jamaica's pride, a symbol of might,
Where champions are made, in the morning light!
From track and field, to football and more,
The National Stadium, is a place to adore!

Did you know, that it hosted the World Championships too,
In 2009, the world came, to see Jamaica's crew!
Usain Bolt, and Shelly-Ann, made history here,
Their world records, still bring cheer!

The stadium's lights, shine bright at night,
A beacon of hope, a guiding light!
For athletes and fans, it's a special place,
Where dreams are made, and memories embrace!

So let's visit the National Stadium, and cheer,
For Jamaica's athletes, and the records they hold dear!
A symbol of pride, a place of delight,
The National Stadium, shining so bright!

The energy's electric, the atmosphere's grand,
When Jamaica's athletes, take to the land!
With every jump, and every sprint,
The crowd erupts, in a joyful shout!

From young to old, it's a place to behold,
Where heroes are made, and stories unfold!
So come and experience, the thrill and the might,
Of the National Stadium, shining so bright!

Let's celebrate, this iconic place,
Where the Jamaican spirit shines on every face!
With pride and joy, we'll cheer and chant,
For the National Stadium, a true Jamaican gem,
in every way, a champion

GIRLS CHAMPS: WHERE QUEENS ARE CROWNED

In Jamaica's land of sun and delight,
Girls Champs is the place, where athletes shine so bright!
Every year, they gather, to run, jump and play,
Showcasing their talent, in a joyful way!

From St. Jago to Wolmer's, and all schools in between,
The girls come together, to compete and be seen!
With sprinting, distance, and relays too,
They push themselves hard, their best they do!

Did you know, that Shelly-Ann Fraser-Pryce, the great,
Competed in Girls Champs, before her Olympic fate?
She set records, that still stand today,
A true legend, in every single way!

The crowd cheers on, with a happy sound,
As the girls give their all, on the track, where they're found!
With every race, a new champion's crowned,
And the crowd erupts, in a joyful sound!

Girls Champs is a celebration, of girls' power and might,
A time for friends, fun and play, with delight!
So let's cheer on the girls, and their amazing feats,
As they shine so bold, in the Jamaican heat!

BOYS CHAMPS: A CELEBRATION OF SPEED

In Jamaica's land of sun and fun,
Where athletes gather, everyone!
Boys Champs is the place to be,
A showcase of talent, for all to see!

Held every year, in March's warm light,
The best of the best, compete with all their might,
In events like sprinting, distance, and more,
They push themselves hard, to be the ultimate score!

From Calabar to Clarendon College too,
The schools come together, to see who's best, it's true,
With relay teams, and individual stars,
They shine so bright, like a work of art!

The crowd cheers on, with a joyful sound,
As the athletes give their all, on the track, where they're found,
With every race, a story unfolds,
Of dedication, hard work, and a heart of gold!

Did you know, that Usain Bolt, the great,
Competed in Boys Champs, before his Olympic fate?
He set records, that still stand today,
A true legend, in every single way!

The excitement builds, as the days go by,
As the athletes strive, to reach the top, they try,
With each event, a new champion's crowned,
And the crowd erupts, in a happy sound!

Boys Champs is more, than just a meet,
It's a celebration, of youth, and their unique feat,
So let's cheer on, the boys, and their might,
As they shine so bright, in the Jamaican light.

REGGAE BOYZ: ONE OF A KIND!

In Jamaica's land of wood and water,
Where music and soccer come together,
There's a team that's loved by all,
The Reggae Boyz, standing tall!

With jerseys gold, green and black,
They play their hearts out, and never slack,
Their passion and skill on full display,
Making Jamaica proud every single day!

From Leon Bailey to Andre Blake too,
The Reggae Boyz have made their mark it's true,
In World Cups and tournaments, they've played with might,
And brought joy to their fans, shining so bright!

Their music and moves, a wondrous sight,
Like a synchronized dance, so tight and bright,
The Reggae Boyz, a team of delight,
Filling hearts with cheer, morning, noon, and night!

With every pass, shot, and goal,
They give their all, with heart and soul,
Their love for soccer, a beacon of light,
Guiding them forward, through day and night!

From the hills of Kingston to the beaches of Negril,
The Reggae Boyz are loved by all, it's a thrill,
Their spirit and talent, a treasure to see,
A shining star, for you and me!

Their rhythm and flow, like a sweet melody,
Makes us want to dance, wild and free,
The Reggae Boyz, a symphony of delight,
Filling our lives with joy, pure and bright!

So let's cheer on the Reggae Boyz with glee,
And celebrate their spirit, wild and free,
For they are the pride of Jamaica's land,
And their love for soccer, ever so grand!

JAMAICAN SCHOOLS

Jamaican schools, a place to learn,
Where children grow and knowledge is earned.
From math to reading, to science and more,
A foundation for life, forever in store.

Teachers guide with a gentle hand,
Helping students learn and understand.
With encouragement and support, they lead the way,
Helping their students shine, come what may.

Jamaican schools, a place to play,
Where friendships grow in a joyful way.
Recess, sports, and music too—
A well-rounded education for me and you.

From early years to high school and beyond,
Jamaican schools, a journey so strong.
Preparing students for the future ahead,
Equipping them with skills for life's path, they said.

Jamaican schools, a source of pride,
Where children shine and reach their full stride.
With a strong foundation in education so true,
Jamaican schools—a place where dreams come through!

Arts and culture, an important part,
Of Jamaican schools, a creative art.
Music and dance, and art so bright,
A celebration of talent, a pure delight.

Libraries and labs, and computers too,
Helping students learn, with technology new.
Research and discovery, a path to explore,
In the digital age, innovations galore!

Jamaican schools, a place to grow,
Where children blossom, and their futures glow.
With a strong education, and a heart so true,
Jamaican schools, a place for dreams to come through!

NEXT STEP: TERTIARY EDUCATION

In Jamaica's land of wood and water bright,
Tertiary education shines with delight!
From colleges to universities, a path is laid,
For young minds to grow, and futures to be made.

The University of the West Indies, a premier place,
Where minds are opened, and knowledge fills the space!
With campuses in Mona, and Montego Bay too,
UWI's the spot where dreams come true!

The College of Agriculture, Science and Education,
In Portland's hills, a gem of great education!
From farming to science, and teaching with flair,
CASE's graduates are truly beyond compare!

The University of Technology, in Kingston's heart,
Where innovation meets art, and technology takes part!
With programs in engineering, computing, and more,
UTech's students are Jamaica's future score!

So if you're a young Jamaican, with a dream to pursue,
Tertiary education the path that's waiting for you!
With these great colleges and universities in sight,
Your future's bright, and shining with delight!

The Edna Manley College, of Visual and Performing Arts,
Where creativity flows, and talent never departs!
From music to dance, to art and design,
The students are truly one of a kind!

The Northern Caribbean University, in Mandeville's nest,
Where knowledge and faith are deeply invested!
With programs in business, education, and more,
NCU's graduates are Jamaica's future in store!

So come and join the journey, of tertiary education's might,
In Jamaica's colleges and universities, shining so bright!
With knowledge and skills, you'll soar to great heights,
And make Jamaica proud, with all your might!

UWI: A HUB OF LEARNING AND GROWTH

In the Caribbean, where the sun shines bright,
There's a university, that's a wonderful sight.
The University of the West Indies, a name so bold,
With campuses in Jamaica, Barbados, and Trinidad I'm told.

Founded in 1948, with a mission so grand,
To provide education, to the Caribbean land.
With faculties in arts, science, and more,
UWI's the place where knowledge is in store.

The Mona Campus, in Jamaica's capital city,
Is the largest campus, with a vibrant community.
Students from far and wide, come to learn and grow,
With top-notch professors, who help them glow.

UWI's research centers, are making waves so bright,
In fields like medicine, engineering, and environmental
science - right.
They're finding solutions, to the world's big problems too,
With innovation and creativity, they're seeing it through.

So if you're a young scholar, with a dream to pursue,
The University of the West Indies, is a great place to break
through!

With its rich history, and academic excellence so high,
UWI's the perfect place to reach for the stars and fly!

The university's alumni, are a proud and talented crew,
With achievements in many fields, they're making a
difference too.
From leaders in government, to innovators in tech,
UWI's graduates are shining bright, with a spirit that
connects.

UWI's campus life, is vibrant and fun,
With clubs and organisations, for everyone!
From sports to culture, to community service too,
There's something for every interest, at UWI, it's true!

So come and experience, the UWI spirit so bright,
Where knowledge and fun come together in delight!
With its warm Caribbean setting, and academic excellence
so high,
The University of the West Indies is a wonderful place to
fly!

UTECH: THE HEART OF JAMAICA'S TECH SCENE

In Jamaica's capital city, where innovation reigns,
There's a university that's making a name.
University of Technology, a place to learn and grow,
Where technology and science, are the keys to know.

Founded in 1958, with a mission so grand,
To provide education, in technology's land.
With faculties in engineering, computing, and more,
UTech's the place, where innovation soars.

The campus is buzzing, with students so bright,
Working on projects, day and night.
From robots to apps, to sustainable energy too,
UTech's students are creating, a future anew.

UTech's research centres, are making waves so bold,
In fields like renewable energy, and technology to hold.
They're finding solutions, to the world's big problems too,
With innovation and creativity, they're seeing it through.

The university's alumni, are a proud and talented crew,
With achievements in many fields, they're making a
difference it's true.

From innovators in tech, to leaders in government too
UTech's graduates are shining bright, with a spirit that
shines through

UTech's campus life, is vibrant and fun
With clubs and organisations, for everyone!
From sports to culture, to community service too
There's something for every interest, at UTech, too!

The university's partnerships, with industry so strong
Help students gain experience, where they belong
With internships and mentorship, they're prepared to
succeed
In the world of technology, where innovation is the key

So come and experience, the UTech spirit so bright
Where innovation and learning come together in delight!
With its rich history, and academic excellence so high
The University of Technology is a wonderful place to fly!

PROFESSIONS IN JAMAICA: A RHYMING CELEBRATION

In Jamaica's land of wood and water bright,
There are many professions that shine with delight!
From doctors to teachers, to engineers too,
Each one is important, and helps our country grow for true.

Doctors and nurses, with skills so fine,
Help keep us healthy, and make us shine!
They work in hospitals, and clinics with care,
And make sure we're well, with a smile to share.

Teachers and professors, with knowledge so grand,
Help us learn and grow, in this beautiful land!
They teach us maths, science, and language with flair,
And help us discover our talents that's there.

Engineers and architects, with skills so neat,
Design and build bridges, and roads so great!
They make sure our buildings, are safe and strong,
And help our country grow, all day long.

Lawyers and judges, with justice in sight,
Help keep our country fair, and make things right!
They work in courts, and offices here,
And make sure we're safe, with a system that's fair.

Farmers and fishermen, with hard work and might,
Grow and catch our food, making everything right!
They work in fields, and on the sea with care,
And make sure we have food to eat and share.

Artists and musicians, with creativity so bright,
Make us smile and dance, with their talents all night!
They paint and play music, with passion and fire,
And make our country rich, with cultural desire.

So let's appreciate, these professions so fine,
And thank them for their work in making Jamaica shine!
Each one is important, and helps our country grow,
And we're lucky to have them, don't you know!

JAMAICAN POLITICS IN ACTION: A POEM FOR YOUNG MINDS

In Jamaica's land of wood and water bright,
Politics plays a role, day and night.
From leaders to lawmakers, they work with care,
To make decisions, that show they're always there.

The Prime Minister's role, is a big one to fill,
Leading the country, with a gentle will.
Andrew Holness, is the current PM's name,
Working hard for Jamaica is his aim.

The Parliament's where, laws are made with ease,
Senators and MPs, work together with expertise.
They debate and discuss, with passion and fire,
To create laws that make Jamaica – that's their one desire.

Jamaica's political parties, are two in number,
The JLP and PNP work together.
They may have differences, but they work as a team,
To make Jamaica great, is their ultimate dream.

So let's learn about politics, and its role in our land,
It's important to know how it works hand in hand.
With leaders and lawmakers, working together with care,
Jamaica's future's bright, and its politics is dear!

The Governor-General, represents the King with grace,
A symbolic role that shows Jamaica's history and pace.
Sir Patrick Allen, is the current GG's name,
Working hard for Jamaica is his aim.

Local government, is important too,
Parish councils and mayors, work hard for me and you.
They fix roads and schools, and make sure we're safe,
Local government is vital in the race.

So let's respect our leaders, and the work they do,
They're working hard for Jamaica, for me and you.
Politics is important, don't you know,
It shapes our country, and helps us grow!

JAMAICAN FOOD

Jamaican food, a culinary delight,
Flavours, spices and colours, oh what sweet sight.
From jerk chicken to curry goat,
Our food is a fusion, that can't be beat.
Ackee and saltfish, a breakfast treat,
Fruits and veggies, that can't be beat.
Callaloo and yams, a flavorful mix,
Jamaican food, is a tasty fix.
Rice and peas, a side dish so fine,
Fried dumplings and festival, oh so divine.
Jamaican patties, a snack so sweet,
Our food is a treasure, that can't be beat.
Jamaican food, is a cultural blend,
African, British, and Spanish, a true friend.
Our food is a reflection, of our history and pride,
A delicious legacy, that we can't hide.
So come and taste, our Jamaican delight,
Flavours and spices, that will excite.
Your taste buds will dance, with joy and glee,
Jamaican food, a treat for you and me!

JAMAICAN FRUITS

In Jamaica's fields, a colourful sight,
Fruits grow in abundance, a true delight.
Mangoes sweet, and juicy too,
A favourite fruit, for me and you.

Pineapples prickly, on the outside so bright,
But inside so sweet, a flavorful bite.
Grown in the hills, where the soil is rich,
A fruit so versatile, in every dish.

Coconuts tall, with shells so strong,
A source of milk, where recipes belong.
In soups, in stews, or just to drink,
A refreshing treat, with a tropical blink.

Papayas soft, with a buttery flesh,
A fruit so nutritious, with a healthy mesh.
Vitamins and minerals, in every bite,
A snack so wholesome, morning, noon, or night.

Oranges, juicy, with a peel so fine,
Grapefruits tart, with a flavour so divine.
They're a great source of vitamin C too,
And they're grown in Jamaica, just waiting for you.

Watermelons refreshing, with a rind so green,
Honeydew sweet, with a flavour so serene.
They're a great snack on a hot summer day,
And they're grown in Jamaica, in a special way.

Mangoes are a favourite, among kids and adults too,
Rich in vitamins and minerals to chew.
They're a great snack, to keep you going strong,
And they're grown in Jamaica, all year long.

Passion fruits tropical, with a pulp so golden,
Star apple purple, with a soft inside like pollen.
They're a great source of vitamins and minerals too,
And they're grown in Jamaica, just waiting for you.

Ackee, soft, with a creamy pride,
Cherries small, with a flavor sweet and wide.
They're a great snack, to keep you going strong,
And they're grown in Jamaica, all year long.

In Jamaica's markets, a rainbow so bright,
Fruits of every kind, a pure delight.
So come and taste, the flavours so true,

Jamaican fruits, a treat for me and you!
With so many choices, your taste buds will cheer,
Jamaican fruits, a snack so healthy, it's clear!

MANGOES:
JAMAICA'S SWEETEST TREASURE

In Jamaica's lush orchards, a sweet delight
Grows ripe and ready, shining bright
Mangoes of all kinds, a colourful sight
A favourite fruit, loved day and night

The East Indian, a popular variety
Sweet and creamy, with no anxiety
The Number Eleven, a mango so fine
Eaten ripe, or used in chutney's divine

The Langra, a mango from India's shore
Brought to Jamaica, and loved evermore
Its flavour unique, a taste so sublime
Eaten fresh, or used in a sweet mango lime

Jamaicans love mangoes, you need to know
In smoothies, salads, or just a snack to go
They're eaten ripe, or used in a sweet preserve
Mango chutney, a condiment to deserve

In Jamaica's markets, a vibrant display
Mangoes of all kinds, in a colourful way
From green to yellow, to orange and red
A rainbow of mangoes, dancing in your head

The season's short, but the joy is long
Mango time in Jamaica, a happy song
So come and taste, the sweetness and delight
Of Jamaica's mangoes, taste buds ignite

In Jamaica's kitchens, a treasured treat
Mangoes are cooked, like a sweet meat
In pies and tarts, or just a simple slice
Mangoes are loved, with every bite

So if you're in Jamaica, during mango time
Make sure to eat some anytime
Your taste buds will dance, with joy and delight
In Jamaica mango time – a pleasure so right!

JAMAICAN SPICES: A FLAVOURFUL SYMPHONY

Jamaican spices, a flavorful blend,
Warming my heart like a true, dear friend.
Cinnamon's warmth, nutmeg's sweet embrace,
Ginger's zing, a spicy, lovely grace.
It's a taste that shines through every bite,
Filling my life with savory delight.

Jamaican spice is a gift so true,
Filling my heart with warmth anew.
Its rich aroma, a sweet perfume,
In every dish, it finds its room.
The scents of allspice, cinnamon grand,
Dance on my tongue, a spicy band.
Nutmeg's touch, a gentle grace,
Makes every meal a joy-filled space.

Jamaican spices, an aromatic treat,
Filling my senses with a soft, sweet beat.
Allspice and thyme, a frequent delight,
Shining so bright, day or night.
They're a cultural cornerstone, a vibrant art,
A culinary pulse, throbbing with heart.
In every dish we share and impart,
Jamaican spices etch memories, a work of art.

JAMAICA'S BLUE MOUNTAIN COFFEE

In Jamaica's hills, where the air is sweet
Grows a special coffee, that can't be beat
Blue Mountain coffee, a treasure so rare
Grown with love and care, in the Jamaican air
A flavour so rich, that's beyond compare

The coffee plants grow, in the misty dawn
Their leaves a vibrant green, their beans a precious spawn
The farmers tend them, with skill and grace
Ensuring each bean has a perfect taste
For the coffee that's made, in this special place

The beans are harvested, with care and with might
Roasted to perfection, in the morning light
Aroma and flavour, that's simply the best
Jamaica Blue Mountain coffee, passes the test
A delight for the senses, that's truly blessed

In the cup, it's a treat, a joy to behold
A flavour so smooth, that never grows old
A delight for the taste buds, a pleasure so true
Jamaica Blue Mountain coffee, is a dream come through
A coffee so special, that's made just for you

So let's raise a cup, to Jamaica's Blue Mountain high
A coffee so special, that touches the sky
A flavour so rich, that's a treasure so rare
Jamaica Blue Mountain coffee, is beyond compare
A delight for the senses - truly fair and square.

JERK CHICKEN

Jerk chicken, a dish so fine,
From Jamaica, where the flavours shine.
Allspice and thyme, an aromatic blend,
Makes your taste buds, want to transcend.
The jerk seasoning, a secret so grand,
A mix of spices, that's rubbed on the land.
On chicken, pork, or tofu too,
It's a flavour, that's loved by me and you.
The allspice tree, a wonder to see,
Grown in Jamaica, a treasure to me.
Its berries and leaves, used in the jerk blend,
Give the chicken, a flavour that never ends.
Jerk chicken, a popular dish worldwide,
Grilled to perfection, it's a taste to blow your mind.
With rice and peas, or roasted sweet potatoes too,
It's a meal, that's loved by me and you.
So if you haven't tried, this Jamaican delight,
Jerk chicken, a flavour so bright.
Give it a go, come take a big bite,
You'll love the flavor, of this Caribbean delight!

ESCOVITCH FISH

Escovitch fish, a dish so delicious and sweet,
From Jamaica, where the flavours meet.
Fresh catch of the day, marinated with care,
In a spicy sauce, that's beyond compare.
The fish is cooked, in a savoury sauce,
With onions and other spices, its taste is boss.
The marinade, a secret blend so pure,
Makes the fish tender, that's for sure.
Escovitch fish, a popular dish on the go,
In Jamaica's restaurants, it's a favourite to know.
Served with bammy, or yams on the side,
It's a meal so delicious, it fills you inside.
The scotch bonnet pepper, a key ingredient so grand,
Adds heat to the dish, makes its flavour expand.
But don't worry, it's not too hot to eat,
The flavours balance, and the heat retreats.
So if you haven't tried, this Jamaican dish as yet,
Escovitch fish, is a taste sensation you won't regret.
So give it a go, and take a big bite,
You'll love the flavours, of this Jamaican delight!

BAMMY

Bammy, a food so traditional and true,
From Jamaica, where the cassava grows in view.
A flatbread made, from the root so fine,
Baked on a griddle, until it's crispy and divine.

Cassava, a staple, in many lands,
Used to make bammy, with a skillful hand.
Peel and grate, then squeeze out the excess,
The starch is removed, and the goodness is amassed.

Bammy is served, with a variety of delight,
Fried fish, stews, or even just butter, oh so right.
A side dish so versatile, it's a pleasure to share,
Bammy's a food, that's beyond compare.

In Jamaica's history, bammy played a big part,
A food for the people, that warmed the heart.
From Taino roots, to African and Spanish too,
Bammy's a fusion, of cultures shining through.

So if you haven't tried, this Jamaican treat,
Bammy's a food, that's great to eat.
So give it a go, and take a big bite,
You'll love the taste, of this Jamaican delight!

BREADFRUIT DELIGHT

In Jamaica's lush hills, a treasure grows,
Breadfruit, a staple, that everyone knows.
A starchy delight, that's versatile too,
Boiled, roasted, or fried; it's a dish for you.

Jamaicans love breadfruit, it's a fact so true,
They eat it for breakfast, lunch, and dinner too.
With ackee and saltfish, it's a classic pair,
A traditional dish, that's beyond compare.

Roasted breadfruit, with a crispy skin,
Is a popular snack, that fills deep within.
Reach of a roadside vendor, or a market stall,
Served with a dash of salt, or a sprinkle that's all.

Boiled breadfruit, with a dash of spice,
Is a side dish, that's always nice.
With a hint of onion, and a sprinkle of thyme,
It's a flavour so good, that's simply sublime.

Fried breadfruit, with a crispy crust,
Is a treat so tasty, that's a must.
With a dip of ketchup, or a sprinkle of cheese,
It's a snack so good, that brings us to our knees.

Jamaicans love breadfruit, in every way,
They eat it daily, come what may.
It's a fruit so versatile, that's a treasure so true,
A staple in Jamaica, that's forever new.

In Jamaica's cuisine, breadfruit plays a part,
A delicious staple, that's in every heart.
So if you're in Jamaica, don't be shy,
Some breadfruit, you must try!

JAMAICAN DRINKS

Jamaican drinks, a refreshing treat,
From the island of wood and water, they can't be beat.
Fresh coconut water, a cooling delight,
Quenching your thirst while out in the light!

Sorrel drink, a sweet and tangy treat,
From the flower of the hibiscus plant, sweet on your teeth.
A Christmas favourite in Jamaica's festive cheer,
A drink so delicious, it's a joy to hold dear.

Pineapple juice, a tropical flavour so sweet,
Grown in Jamaica's fields where the sunbeams meet.
Rich in vitamin C and a taste so divine,
A refreshing drink that's simply sublime.

Ginger beer, a spicy kick so fine,
Made from the root of the ginger plant—let's dine!
Aids digestion and warms the soul,
A drink so comforting, come drink from the bowl.

Mannish water, a drink so unique and bold,
Made from the sap of the coconut tree, so cold.
Rich in electrolytes and a taste so refreshing too,
A drink so revitalizing, it's a joy to renew!

Jamaican rum, a spirit so smooth and warm,
Aged to perfection, in the Caribbean form.
A sip or two, and you'll feel just right,
A drink so enjoyable, on a warm summer night.

Fresh fruit juices, blends so colourful and sweet,
Made from tropical fruits, in Jamaican sun-heat.
Orange, grapefruit, and passion fruit too,
Refreshing drinks, perfect for me and you.

Jamaican drinks, a treasure to behold,
A fusion of flavours, that never grows old.
So come and taste, the island's refreshing delight,
And let the spirit of Jamaica shine with joy and light!

COCONUT SNACKS

Coconut snacks, a tasty delight,
From Jamaica's trees, shining so bright.
Drops and gizzarda, a sweet treat in store,
Made from coconut milk, and a whole lot more.

Coconut drops, a favourite of mine,
Made with coconut milk, and a touch of sugar divine.
Rolled into balls, and baked to perfection,
A snack so delicious, it needs a reaction.

Gizzarda, a snack so crunchy and light,
Made with coconut flakes and spice for everyone's delight.
Fried until crisp, and seasoned with care,
A snack so flavourful, it's a joy to share.

Coconut snacks, a healthy choice so grand,
Rich in fiber, and protein in hand.
Good for your body, and your taste buds too,
A snack so wholesome, it's a joy to chew.

So come and try, these coconut snacks so fine,
Made in Jamaica, of different designs.
You'll savour the flavours, and enjoy them too,
Coconut snacks, for me and you!

JAMAICA'S STORY

Jamaica's history, a tale so grand,
From the Taino people to a new land.
Christopher Columbus arrived on our shore
In 1494, opening a new chapter in store.

The Spanish came with their flags so bright,
But the British took control in a bitter fight.
Sugar plantations, with slaves so dear,
A painful past that brings us to tears.

But we fought for freedom with hearts so bold,
The Maroons, with their stories untold.
Nanny and Sam Sharpe, heroes of our past,
Leading the way to freedom at last.

Emancipation, a new dawn broke
In 1834, igniting a new path to provoke.
Freedom for all in the land so bright,
A beacon of hope, a guiding light.

In 1962, we gained independence so true,
Jamaica, the land of black, green, and gold.
A proud nation, with strength and might,
A place of culture, where dreams take flight.

Jamaica's story, a history so grand,
A land of beauty in this warm and blessed land.
A place of pride, for one and for all,
A country that rises, standing tall.

SIXTY-TWO AND STRONG, JAMAICA'S SONG

Sixty-two years ago, a nation was born,
Jamaica, a land of beauty, with a story to learn.
We gained our independence, and broke free from chains,
And became a country, with a voice that sustains.

Our flag was raised high, with colours bright and bold,
Black, gold, and green, a symbol of our story to be told.
We've had our struggles, but we've always found a way,
To overcome obstacles, and seize a brighter day.

From Alexander Bustamante, to Norman Manley too,
Our leaders have guided us, with visions so true.
We've produced great athletes, like Usain Bolt and Shelly-Ann,
And musicians like Bob Marley, whose legacy lives on and on.

Our culture's rich and diverse, with music, dance, and art,
We've got reggae, ska, and rocksteady, to give our hearts a start.
We're a nation of innovators, with spirits so bright,
We've made our mark on the world, with our creativity and light.

So here's to Jamaica, on our 62nd year,
A nation of pride, with a heart so clear.
We'll keep moving forward, with a spirit so bold,
Jamaica, we salute you, our independence exposed!

We've got the Blue Mountains, and the Caribbean Sea,
A land of beauty, with a charm that's all our own - you
see.
From Negril to Montego Bay, we've got a coast so fine,
And a people so warm, with a hospitality that's truly
divine.

We've got a history, that's rich and long,
From the Taino people, to the present day, we've got a
story to be sung.
We've been through struggles, but we've always found a
way,
To overcome obstacles and not stay dismayed.

So let's raise our flags high, and celebrate with glee,
Jamaica's 62nd year of independence is a milestone to
see!

JAMAICA'S FREEDOM SONG

Jamaica, Jamaica, a land so free,
Gained independence in 1962, history you see.
From British rule, we broke away,
And became a nation, in a brand new way.

Our flag was raised high, on August 6th with pride,
A symbol of our freedom, for all to abide.
Black, gold, and green, our colours shine so bright,
Representing our people, and our struggle for right.

Alexander Bustamante, a hero of our past,
Led the fight for independence, and freedom at last.
Norman Manley, another leader, who played a key role,
Together they worked to make our nation whole.

We're a nation of warriors, with a spirit so bold,
From Marcus Garvey, to Nanny of the Maroons, our stories
unfold.
We fought for our rights, and our freedom we gained,
And now we celebrate, our independence proclaimed.

So let's raise our flags high, and sing with glee,
Jamaica, Jamaica, we're independent, we're free!
We're a nation of pride, with a heart so true,
Jamaica, Jamaica, we love you!

JAMAICA'S ANTHEM

Jamaica's anthem, a song so sweet,
Echoes of freedom, that can't be beat.
Written by Hugh Sherlock, a man of great might,
In 1962, it became our national delight.

The lyrics speak, of our nation's pride,
A people united, side by side.
We stand together, hand in hand,
A nation strong, in our beloved land.

The anthem's melody, a symphony so grand,
Composed by Robert Lightbourne , a master of the land.
It's a call to action, to build and to strive,
For a brighter tomorrow, where all can survive.

We sing of our nation, with hearts full of cheer,
A land of beauty, where love and joy appear.
From the Blue Mountains, to the sea so blue,
Jamaica's anthem, is a song for me and you.

So let's raise our voices, in joyful harmony,
And sing our anthem, with pure ecstasy.
For Jamaica's anthem, is a song of our pride,
A symbol of unity, where love always abides.

ETERNAL FATHER

Eternal Father, we sing to thee,
A song of praise, for our country's glee.
Jamaica's beauty, we proudly hail,
With hearts united, we never fail.

Our nation's flag, with colours bright,
Black, gold, and green, shining with delight.
We stand together, hand in hand,
A people proud, in our beloved land.

We praise thy name, for our freedom won,
From slavery's chains, to a brighter sun.
Our ancestors' struggles, we'll never forget,
Their courage and strength, we'll always be in debt.

We'll work together, for a brighter day,
With love and unity, we'll find our way.
Through trials and tribulations, we'll stand as one,
And build a nation, where all can have fun.

So let's raise our voices, in joyful cheer,
And sing our anthem, loud and clear.
Eternal Father, we'll always adore,
Our beloved Jamaica, forevermore!

JAMAICA'S FLAG

Jamaica's flag waves high in the air,
A symbol of pride, that's fair and square.
Black, gold, and green, a colorful sight,
A flag that represents Jamaica, shining bright.
A flag that unites us, day and night.

Black is for strength, and the people's power,
Gold is for sunshine, in each and every hour.
Green is for hope, and the beautiful land,
A flag that's special, in this wonderful land.
A flag that waves, with a happy hand.

The flag's design is a work of art,
A creation that's unique, and a treasure to start.
The colors mix in a happy way,
A flag that represents Jamaica, every single day.
A flag that's loved, by you and me.

Jamaica's flag waves high and free,
A symbol of freedom, for you and me.
A flag that represents the land we love,
A flag that's cherished, sent from above.
A flag that's Jamaica, a treasure to love.

So let's wave the flag, with joy and cheer,
A symbol of Jamaica, that's always near.
A flag that unites us, and makes us proud,
A flag that's Jamaica, a treasure allowed,
A flag that waves high in a happy crowd.

JAMAICA'S PLEDGE

We pledge our allegiance, our flag so bright,
With colours bold, and a symbol in sight.
The black, gold, and green, a story to tell,
Of a nation proud, and a people who dwell.

In Jamaica's land, of wood and water wide,
We promise to work, side by side.
To build a nation, strong and free,
Where all can live, in harmony.

We vow to uphold, the rights of all,
To respect and love, one and all.
Regardless of race, or creed, or might,
We'll stand together, shining bright.

With hearts united, we'll face the test,
Of building a nation, where all can rest.
In peace and love, we'll find our way,
And brighten Jamaica day by day.

So let's stand tall, and pledge with glee,
To our beloved Jamaica, we'll be true, you'll see.
With hearts and hands, we'll work as one,
For Jamaica's prosperity, we'll have won!

JAMAICAN SMILE

Jamaican smile, so bright and wide,
Warming my heart, lighting up inside.
A beacon of joy, in a world so grand,
Jamaican smile, taking me to a happy land,
Filling my life with a sense of pride.

Jamaican smile, a treasure to see,
A symbol of hope, for you and me.
A ray of sunshine on a cloudy day,
Jamaican smile, chasing all the blues away,
Making my heart feel happy in a lovely way.

Jamaican smile, a work of art,
A masterpiece, that's straight from the heart.
A reflection of love, that's pure and true,
Jamaican smile, a treasure made for you,
Filling my life with a sense of delight.

Jamaican smile, a gift from above,
A reminder of joy, and a labor of love.
A smile that's contagious, and spreads like a flame,
Jamaican smile, making my heart feel the same,
Filling my life with a sense of joy and fame.

Jamaican smile, a treasure so rare,
Filling my heart with a sense of care.
A smile that's genuine, and comes from the heart,
Jamaican smile, a work of art,
Making my life feel like a happy and joyful ride!

JAMAICA'S TRADITIONS

In Jamaica, a land so free,
Traditions are important, you see.
From music to food, to festivals too,
Jamaican culture is rich and true,
A heritage that's strong through and through.

Reggae music fills the air,
A rhythm that's unique, beyond compare.
Bob Marley's legacy lives on,
A cultural icon, forever strong,
With music that inspires, and never grows old.

Jamaican cuisine, a fusion delight,
Jerk chicken and rice, a flavourful bite.
Ackee and saltfish, a breakfast treat,
Fruits and veg, that can't be beat,
A culinary journey, that's fun to repeat.

Festivals and celebrations, a joyful sound,
Carnival and Reggae Sumfest, all around.
Traditional dances, like the ska and sway,
A cultural heritage, that's here to stay,
Can never be denied, in any way.

Jamaican traditions, make me happy always,
A blend of customs, that's here to stay.
Respect and love, for each other we show,
A sense of community, that always glows!

Our culture's rich, with music, dance, and art,
From reggae to ska, our rhythms touch the heart.
We're a nation of innovators, with a spirit so bright,
From science to sports, we shine with all our might.

We're a land of beauty, with mountains and sea,
From Dunn's River Falls, to the beauty of our trees.
We're a nation of resilience, with a heart so strong,
We've faced our challenges, and our spirit keeps moving on.

So here's to Jamaica, our nation so dear,
We celebrate our independence, year after year.
We're proud of our history, and our culture so grand,
Jamaica, Jamaica, we're a nation! Hooray for our land!

JAMAICAN FESTIVAL FUN

Jamaica's festivals are a sight to see,
A celebration of culture, music and glee!
From Reggae Sumfest to Carnival's delight,
Jamaica's festivals shine with joy and light.

Reggae Sumfest a festival that's truly grand,
Showcasing Jamaica's music, a treasure to expand.
Held in Montego Bay, it's a party all night,
With reggae and dancehall, everything's all right!

Carnival's a festival that's full of colour and fun,
A parade of costumes, music, and dancing in the sun.
From Kingston to Ocho Rios, it's a celebration so bright,
A showcase of Jamaica's culture, a pure delight!

Jamaica Jazz and Blues Festival a treat for the ears,
A celebration of music that brings cheers and cheers.
Held in Kingston, it's a festival that's truly unique,
Showcasing Jamaica's jazz and blues, a musical technique!

Emancipation Day's a festival that's truly important,
A celebration of freedom, a story to be told and retold.
Held on August 1st, it's a day of reflection and pride,
A celebration of Jamaica's history, a story when I heard I
cried.

Rebel Salute a festival that's truly cool,
A celebration of roots reggae, a musical rule.
Held in St. Ann, it's a festival that's truly sweet,
Showcasing Jamaica's music, a treat to repeat.

Jamaica's festivals are a joy to behold,
A celebration of culture, music, and stories untold.
From music to dance, to food and fun,
Jamaica's festivals are a celebration for everyone!

So come and experience Jamaica's festivals for yourself,
A celebration of culture, music, and wealth.
You'll leave with memories that will last all year,
And a heart full of joy, and a spirit of cheer!

JAMAICAN MUSIC

Jamaican music is so sweet,
Making me want to move my feet.
Reggae rhythms, a happy treat,
Jamaican music can't be beat,
Making me feel happy every time I repeat.

Jamaican music is a special sound,
Filling my heart with joy all around.
Drums and bass, a perfect blend,
Jamaican music, my best friend,
Making me feel happy 'til the very end.

Jamaican music is full of life,
Making me want to sing and thrive.
Guitars and keyboards, a beautiful sight,
Jamaican music, shining so bright,
Making me feel happy, filled with delight.

Jamaican music is a treasure to hear,
Filling my heart with joy and cheer.
Jamaican spirit, shining bold and clear,
Jamaican music, a joy to hold dear,
Making me feel happy, year after year.

Jamaican music is a gift to me,
Filling my heart with joy and glee.
Jamaican culture, rich and fun,
Jamaican music, a treasure for everyone,
Making me feel happy all day long!

REGGAE RHYTHM

Music beats, my feet move fast,
Reggae rhythm, that's gonna last.
Jamaican vibes, that'll never grow old,
Making me dance, young and bold.
Feeling happy, never cold.

Drums beating, bass so sweet,
Reggae music, can't be beaten.
I move my body to the rhythm and sound,
Feeling carefree, happiness abound.
Reggae rhythm, all around.

Reggae music takes me away
To a place where I can play.
No worries, no stress, just fun and games,
Reggae rhythm, that's my aim,
Feeling happy, feeling the flame.

Reggae music, that's my soul's delight,
Making me dance through day and night.
I'll keep on moving to the rhythm and beat,
Reggae rhythm, that's my treat,
Feeling happy, feeling complete.

JAMAICAN DANCEHALL

Jamaican dancehall is so much fun,
Dancing and music, for everyone!
Moving and grooving, all day long,
Jamaican dancehall, singing a happy song,
Making me feel happy, all day long.

Jamaican dancehall is a special place,
Where music and dance fill up the space.
Rhythmic beats make me want to play,
Jamaican dancehall, every single day,
Making me feel happy, in a fun way.

Jamaican dancehall is full of energy,
Making me want to dance and be free.
Music and dance, a perfect pair,
Jamaican dancehall, showing we care,
Making me feel happy, without a single scare.

Jamaican dancehall, a cultural expression,
Music and dance, a true obsession.
Rhythmic beats, a dancing thrill,
Jamaican dancehall, a skill to fulfill,
Filling my life, with a joyful will.

Jamaican dancehall is a gift to me,
Filling my heart with joy and spree.
Jamaican culture, rich and fun,
Jamaican dancehall, a treasure for everyone,
Making me feel happy, all day long!

JAMAICAN NIGHTS

Jamaican nights, a mystical spell,
Stars aligning, a story to tell.
Soft breeze whispers, a gentle hue,
Jamaican nights, a dream come true,
Filling my heart with warmth anew.

Jamaican nights, a canvas so grand,
Painted with colours of a vibrant land.
Moonlight glistening on the sea so bright,
Jamaican nights, a pure delight,
Filling my soul with a sense of wonder and light.

Jamaican nights, a rhythm so sweet,
Music and laughter, a treat to repeat.
Drums and bass, a pulsing beat,
Jamaican nights, a dancing treat,
Filling my life with joy and heat.

Jamaican nights, a treasure so rare,
Filling my heart with a sense of care.
A night of peace, under the stars so bright,
Jamaican nights, a pure delight,
Filling my life with love and light!

JAMAICAN GAMES

Hopscotch, jump rope, and tag, oh my!
Games we played outside, 'til the sun said goodbye.
We drew shapes on the ground, with chalk so bright,
And hopped on one foot, with pure delight.

Marbles was another game, we loved to play,
Rolling them down hills, on a sunny day.
We kept them in bags, with colours so bold,
And traded them with friends, a joy untold.

Hide and seek, was a favourite too,
Hiding behind trees, or in a bush or two.
We counted to ten, while our friends hid away,
And sought them out, in a happy, playful way.

Red Rover, Red Rover, let someone come through,
A classic game, that we loved to do.
We held hands in a line, and tried to break through,
But the other team's grip, was strong and true!

Outdoor games, were a joy to play,
Making memories, that never fade away.
So let's go outside, and have some fun,
And play games that, bring us joy, everyone!

Duck, duck, goose, was another delight,
Walking around, in the warm sun's light.
We tapped each other's heads, with a grin so wide,
And ran around, with joyful stride.

Sardines, was a game, we loved to play at night,
Hiding in the dark, with a flashlight's light.
We searched for each other, with a giggle and glee,
And found each other, in a happy family.

Blind man's bluff, was a game, we loved to play,
Covering our eyes, and stumbling along the way.
We tried to catch each other, with a laugh and a shout,
And tagged each other, then gave a shout!

BEATS OF RESILIENCE

In concrete jungles, they rise and fall,
Young hearts beating, with hopes and fears enthralled.
Ghetto streets, a challenging terrain,
Where dreams are made and sometimes strained.
With every step, a story unfolds,
Of resilience, in faces bold.
Eyes that shine, like stars in the night,
Reflecting the strength of their inner light.
Their voices whisper tales of strife,
Of hunger, hardship, and the will to thrive.
Yet amidst the struggle, they find a way
To laugh, to love, to seize the day.
In makeshift parks, they play and roam,
Finding solace in the rhythm of their home.
From dub to reggae, the beat goes on,
A symphony of hope, where they belong.
Ghetto youth, with spirits so bright,
Deserve a chance to shine with all their might.
May their voices be heard, may their stories be told,
And may their dreams, like roses, forever unfold.
Through the cracks of pavement, they sprout and grow,
A testament to life that refuses to let go.
In the face of adversity, they find a way to thrive,
And in their hearts, a fire burns that will forever survive.
May we listen to their stories untold,
And support their journey as they unfold.
For in their strength, we find our own,
And together, we can build a brighter dawn.

JAMAICAN SPIRIT

Jamaican spirit, a fiery flame,
Burning bright and bold, with a passionate claim.
A heart of courage, with a will so strong,
Jamaican spirit, all day long,
Filling my life with a sense of right and wrong.

Jamaican spirit, a creative spark,
Igniting imagination, like a work of art.
A mind of innovation, with a vision so grand,
Jamaican spirit, taking a stand,
Filling my heart with a sense of pride and plan.

Jamaican spirit, a resilient heart,
Beating with determination, from the very start.
A soul of perseverance, with a will to succeed,
Jamaican spirit, indeed,
Filling my life with a sense of purpose and speed.

Jamaican spirit, a shining light,
Guiding me forward, through day and night.
A beacon of hope, with a spirit so bright,
Jamaican spirit, my heart's delight,
Filling my life with joy and light!

ISLAND VIBES

Jamaican vibes, they take me high,
Reggae music, touching the sky.
Drums and bass, a perfect blend,
Feeling irie, with my friends.
Good times rolling, 'til the end.

Rastafarian spirit, shining bright,
One love, one heart, everything's alright.
God's guidance, we never forget,
Respect and unity, we won't regret.
Island vibes, forever set.

Jamaican culture, rich and bold,
Traditions and stories, yet untold.
Music and dance, a beautiful sight,
Feeling the rhythm, day and night.
Island vibes, pure delight.

Reggae legends, like Bob Marley too,
Inspiring us with their message anew.
Love and redemption, in every song,
Jamaican vibes, all day strong.
Forever in our hearts, their legacy lives on.

Island vibes, a treasure so rare,
Jamaican spirit, we proudly share.
Music and love, a perfect pair,
Feeling the vibes, without a care.
Island vibes, beyond compare.

HOUSES IN JAMAICA

Houses in Jamaica, a sight to see,
Colourful and vibrant, as bright as can be.
From wooden to concrete, to brick and stone,
A variety of styles, all their own.

Some have verandas, where you can sit and play,
Watch the sunset, at the end of the day.
Others have gardens, full of flowers so sweet,
A beautiful place, to rest your feet.

In the hills and mountains, houses are built strong,
Surrounded by nature, with wonderful views.
The air is crisp and clean, with a scent so sweet,
And the sound of silence, can't be beat.

In the cities and towns, houses are built close,
Neighbours are friendly, with a smile and a pose.
Community is important, it's a vital part,
Bringing people together, with a loving heart.

In the countryside, houses are surrounded by green,
Fields of sugarcane, and trees so serene.
A peaceful atmosphere, where nature reigns supreme,
A beautiful place, to live and dream.

In the towns and cities, houses are built with flair,
Architectural styles, that show Jamaicans care.
From Georgian to Victorian, to modern designs so bold,
A testament to Jamaican creativity, forever shown.

Houses in Jamaica, a place to call home,
Where love and laughter, are forever sown.
A place to rest, and a place to play,
Houses in Jamaica, a wonderful array.

Houses in Jamaica, a reflection of the past,
A blend of cultures, that forever will last.
A symbol of resilience, and strength so true,
Houses in Jamaica, a story waiting for you!

JAMAICA'S TRANSPORTATION

Jamaica's transportation, a sight to see,
Buses and taxis, moving with glee.
Cars and trucks, on the road they go,
Moving goods and people to and fro.

JUTA buses, a popular sight,
Taking people to their destination so right.
Air-conditioned and comfortable too,
A great way to travel, for me and you.

Taxis and route taxis, a convenient way
To get 'round the island, every single day.
Licensed and safe, with a friendly face,
A great option for transportation, in every place.

Knutsford Express, a luxury ride,
Travelling in style, with comfort inside.
From Kingston to Montego Bay, amenities galore,
And a smooth journey guaranteed for sure.

Bicycles and scooters, a fun way to roam,
Through the streets of Jamaica, with a gentle tone.
A healthy and eco-friendly option, so bright,
A great way to get around, with a sense of delight.

Jamaica's transportation, a network so strong,
Connecting people and places, all day long.
With a variety of options so convenient,
Making travel plans, truly efficient.

FLYING HIGH WITH AIR JAMAICA

Air Jamaica, a symbol of pride,
An airline that was truly one of a kind.
With its red, gold, and blue colours so bright,
A sight to behold, on a bright night.

Founded in 1968, with a mission so grand,
To connect Jamaica to the world's land.
With routes across the Caribbean and beyond,
Air Jamaica's airlines always respond.

From Kingston to New York, to London and more,
Air Jamaica's flights took you to your door.
With comfortable seats, and a friendly crew,
Your journey's a breeze, with Air Jamaica's crew.

Air Jamaica's fleet, was modern and new,
With aircrafts so safe and comfortable too.
The airline's motto, " One Vision, One Caribbean, One
Airline,"
Reflected Jamaica's spirit, a work of art.

So if you were flying high, or flying low,
Air Jamaica was the airline; the way to go!
With its rich history, and service so fine,
Air Jamaica, the airline, was truly divine.

But now, Air Jamaica's wings are still,
No longer flying, against the wind's will.
In 2015, the airline ceased operations, it's true,
A sad day for Jamaica, and its aviation crew.

The reasons were many, the costs were high,
The competition fierce, the airline said goodbye.
But memories remain, of its proud past,
A legacy lives on, forever to last.

Though Air Jamaica's gone, its spirit remains,
In the hearts of Jamaicans, and aviation's gains.
A new airline rose, Caribbean Airlines took flight,
Connecting Jamaica to the world, with all its might.

JAMAICA'S ECONOMIC BEAT

Welcome to Jamaica's economic quest,
Where entrepreneurship and innovation
 are truly the best!
We grow sugarcane, bananas, and more,
Exporting them worldwide,
to meet global demand for sure!
We're a hub for trade,
with ports that bustle and thrive,
Connecting the Caribbean, with the world alive.
Tourism is booming, visitors flock to our shore,
For reggae music, beautiful beaches,
and culture galore!
We create art and music, that inspire and delight,
Selling them to visitors,
 who appreciate our creative might.
Jamaica's economy is on the move,
innovating every day,
With entrepreneurs and inventors, leading the way!
We're building a future, that's bright and bold,
With opportunities for all, young and old.
Our economy is diverse, with sectors that thrive,
From agriculture to tech,
we're making strides and rising high.
We're a nation of innovators, with a spirit that's free,
Creating a prosperous future, full of glee!

JAMAICA'S MONEY

In 1962, Jamaica got its say,
To pay for things, in a brand new way.
The pound and shilling were used with glee,
But then came the dollar, for you and me.
A new era began, in the economy,
The Jamaican dollar was introduced with pride.
Replaced the pound, it stepped aside,
Coins were minted, with symbols so bright.
Like the hummingbird, and the crocodile in sight,
A new currency, for day and night.
Notes were printed, with faces so dear,
Like Marcus Garvey, and Norman Manley clear.
Their contributions, to Jamaica's growth and might,
Honoured on money, shining so bright.
A tribute to heroes, in plain sight,
As time went on, new notes were added too.
Like the $500, and the $1000, brand new,
And even a $5000 bill, for big transactions too.
Jamaica's money, grew and grew,
A convenient way, to pay and do.
Jamaica's money, is used every day,
To buy and sell, in a fun and easy way.
It's a part of life, in Jamaica's land
Helping us trade, hand to hand
Making life easier, for you and me!

FORGIVE

In the corner of the family, it is inevitable to have
friction,
Small quarrels and misunderstandings, frequent?
But forgiveness, like the warmth of the sun,
It can break down barriers and mend hearts.

Let go of those resentments, cherish each other's love,
Let understanding and tolerance become our partners.
When the heart is freed and the intimate connection is
restored,
As if back in the past, feel the warmth of home.

Everybody makes mistakes, everybody gets lost,
But gentle forgiveness is the bond of family.
Planting seeds of hope in each other's lives,
Let love in the future bloom with endless glory.

So let us learn, to bravely let go,
And trust that new beginnings will grow,
For in release, we find the strength to know,
And the courage to start anew, and make it so.

UNBREAKABLE: THIS IS ME!

In a land that's far from my sunny home,
I stand my ground, no need to roam.
A Jamaican heart, proud and free,
Facing struggles that challenge me.

Racism's shadow looms so large,
Judged by color, scars they carve.
But in my soul, a fire bright,
Just like a beacon in the darkest night.

Rejection comes with stinging pain,
Yet through it all, I remain.
For every no, I'll find my yes,
My spirit's strength, I must confess.

Discrimination, harsh and cold,
Tries to break me, tries to take its hold.
But roots run deep, they keep me strong,
In this foreign land, I belong.

With every step, I rise anew,
A testament to what I do.
From Kingston's shores to distant lands,
I build my dreams with my own hands.

This is me, unbowed, unbent,
A soul of courage, never spent.
Through struggles, tears, and victory,
A Jamaican heart, wild and free.

WE FALL, WE RISE

We rise on eagle's wings, so high and free,
Our spirits soaring, wild and carefree.
We dance on sunbeams, with hearts full of cheer,
Our laughter echoing, without a fear.

But then we fall, like autumn's leaves from trees,
Our dreams shattered, our hearts on our knees.
We search for answers, in the dark of night,
Our souls struggling, to find the light.

We rise again, like phoenix from the ash,
Our resilience, a beacon to clash.
With every fall, we learn and grow,
Our strength and courage, forever to glow.

We rise and fall, like the ebb and flow,
Of the ocean's tides, our journey to know.
We rise and fall, like the sun and the moon,
Our lives a rhythm, a symphony in tune.

We rise and fall, but never give up the fight,
For in the rising, we shine with all our light.
And in the falling, we learn to be strong,
We rise and fall, but our spirit keeps moving on.

www.ingramcontent.com/pod-product-compliance
Lightning Source LLC
Chambersburg PA
CBRC090824120626
46547CB00007B/598